The Boy
Who Invented
TV

The Boy
Who Invented
TV

The Story of
Philo Farnsworth

BY KATHLEEN KRULL

ILLUSTRATED BY GREG COUCH

DRAGONFLY BOOKS • NEW YORK

To Ethan Brewer, future inventor.
—K.K.

To Karen with love.
Thank you.
—G.C.

Endpaper television photographs courtesy:
www.tvhistory.tv/, www.vintagetvsets.com, and www.harryposter.com

All rights reserved. Published in the United States by Dragonfly Books, an imprint of
Random House Children's Books, a division of Random House LLC, a Penguin Random House
Company, New York. Originally published in hardcover in the United States by Alfred A. Knopf,
an imprint of Random House Children's Books, New York, in 2009.

Dragonfly Books with the colophon is a registered trademark of Random House LLC.

Visit us on the Web! randomhouse.com/kids

Educators and librarians, for a variety of teaching tools, visit us at RHTeachersLibrarians.com

The Library of Congress has cataloged the hardcover edition of this work as follows:
Krull, Kathleen.
The boy who invented TV: the story of Philo Farnsworth / by Kathleen Krull. — 1st ed.
p. cm.
Includes bibliographical references.
ISBN 978-0-375-84561-1 (trade) — ISBN 978-0-375-94561-8 (lib. bdg.)
1. Farnsworth, Philo Taylor, 1906–1971—Juvenile literature. 2. Inventors—United States—
Biography—Juvenile literature. 3. Television—History—Juvenile literature. I. Title.
TK6635.F3K78 2009 621.3880092—dc22 [B] 2008035500

ISBN 978-0-385-75557-3 (pbk.)

MANUFACTURED IN CHINA

10 9 8 7 6 5

First Dragonfly Books Edition

Life Before Philo

Imagine what it was like growing up on a farm in the American

West of 1906. With electricity rare out in the country, chores took up most of your day. No refrigerators, no cars, few phones, hardly any indoor bathrooms. Long distances separated you from friends and relations. Meeting up with others took some effort—you rode a horse or walked. There were trains, but riding or even seeing one was a big deal.

Getting news was another challenge. What government leaders were doing in Washington, the latest in the arts and sciences, whether sports teams were winning or losing, new information of any kind—it trickled in haphazardly by mail. Not many people had books, and libraries were few and far between.

It was all a bit lonely.

What about fun? Movies—no. Radio—no (it was only on military ships). There was music, if you played your own instruments. There were no malls to go hang out at. When you had enough money saved up to buy a bicycle or roller skates, you ordered from the "wish book"—the Sears, Roebuck mail-order catalog.

And there was no television. That's right. **NO TV**.

In 1906, inside a log cabin on a farm in Utah, a boy was born who would change things. His name was Philo Taylor Farnsworth.

No sooner did Philo Farnsworth learn to talk than he asked a question. Then another, and another. His parents answered as best they could.

Noticing Philo's interest in anything mechanical, his father took the three-year-old boy to see a train at a station. At first Philo was afraid this huge, noisy thing might be a monster. But the nice engineer invited the boy up into the cab with him, explaining a bit about how steam-powered trains worked.

That night Philo sat at the kitchen table and drew detailed pictures of what went on inside the motor of a train.

Two new machines captivated Philo as he grew up. One was a hand-cranked telephone, purchased by a neighbor. Holding the phone one day, hearing the voice of his beloved aunt, six-year-old Philo got goose bumps. After all, she lived a long ways away!

Another neighbor brought a hand-cranked phonograph to a dance. Music swirling out of a machine—it was almost impossible to believe.

"These things seemed like magic to me," Philo said later. Besides being incredibly clever, the inventions brought people together in whole new ways.

Philo's father shared his wonder. On clear summer nights, as they lay in the grass and gazed at the stars, his father told him about Alexander Graham Bell and the telephone, Thomas Edison and the phonograph. Inventors—these became Philo's heroes.

Away on a temporary job, his father appointed Philo, the oldest of five children, the "man" in the family. Philo was eight. His many chores included feeding the pigs, milking and grazing the cow, fetching wood for the stove. He did get his own pony—Tippy.

It was also a sort of reward to skip school for a while. Bullies there teased him about his unusual name. Shy and serious, Philo didn't fight back.

He found it far more appealing to practice reading with his grandmother's Sears, Roebuck catalog. It had toys . . . as well as cameras, alarm clocks, and machines that used a new, invisible source of power. Electricity, it was called.

In his spare time, Philo raised lambs and sold them. When he had enough money saved up, he visited his grandmother to pick a bicycle out of her catalog.

But somehow, she talked him into ordering a violin instead. Philo did love the sound of music, its orderly rhythms. And even at age ten, he dreamed of fame. Maybe he could find it by creating music like what he heard on the neighbor's phonograph.

Soon he was performing in dance bands, making five dollars every Friday night.

Playing the violin was one more thing for the bullies to tease him about. Then one day Philo fought back, and the teasing ended.

Trying for a better life, the Farnsworths moved from Utah to an Idaho farm with fields of beets and potatoes. Eleven-year-old Philo drove one of their covered wagons, carrying a crate of piglets, a cage of hens, his violin, and their new prize possession— a phonograph.

Arriving in the Snake River Valley, he noticed something up in the air—power lines. Their new home was wired for electricity! A generator ran the lights and water heater, the hay stacker and grain elevator, and other farm equipment.

And up in the attic was another welcome surprise. A shelf of old popular-science magazines, with thrilling articles about magnetism, electricity, and those new "magic boxes"—radios. Philo promptly claimed this as his bedroom. His chores began before dawn, but he trained himself to wake an hour early so he could switch on the light and read in bed. Any spare money he had went to buy more magazines.

That's when he saw the word "television" for the first time. It meant a machine that was something like a radio, only it sent pictures instead of sounds.

It didn't actually exist yet, but scientists were racing to invent one.

The electric generator broke down a lot, and repairs were costly. Each time the repairman came, Philo bombarded him with questions.

After yet another breakdown, Philo set out to fix the machine himself. He took it apart, cleaned it, put it back together, and pressed the "on" button. It worked.

Philo's father was enormously proud of him. From then on, he was the Farnsworths' electrical engineer.

Philo tinkered with broken motors, reels of wire, old tools. He devised gadgets to hook up to the generator— anything to make his chores easier, like installing lights in the barn.

His least favorite thing was washing clothes—hours of standing while pushing and pulling the lever that swished the water around the washtub. So he attached a motor with pulleys to the lever to make it churn on its own, leaving him extra time to read.

When he was thirteen, Philo entered a contest sponsored by *Science and Invention* magazine. Using what he'd learned about magnets, he pictured an ignition lock that would make the new Model T Fords harder to steal.

When he won the contest, Philo spent the prize money on his first pair of proper long pants. Wearing boyish short pants at the Friday dances was just plain embarrassing.

Philo went on investigating television. An article called "Pictures that Fly Through the Air" stimulated him. Scientists were having no luck—so far their ideas resulted in crude mechanical devices that used whirling disks and mirrors.

Philo doubted any disk could whirl fast enough to work. Much better to do the job electronically. To harness electrons, those mysterious, invisible particles that traveled at the speed of light . . .

Pictures that Fly Through the Air

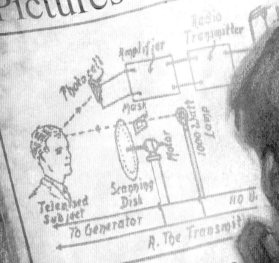

Though it may see~~m~~
far-fetched, scienti~~sts~~
trying for years

...practical application
...~~n~~ew ways of splitting
...pictures into electrons

One bright, sunny day, fourteen-year-old Philo plowed
the potato fields. It was the best chore for thinking—
out in the open country by himself. Back and forth, back
and forth . . . the plow created rows of overturned earth.
He looked behind him at the lines he was carving—
perfectly parallel.

Then he almost fell off the plow seat. All his thoughts fused together. Instead of seeing rows of dirt, he saw a way to create television: breaking down images into parallel lines of light, capturing them and transmitting them as electrons, then reassembling them for a viewer. If it was done quickly enough, people's eyes could be tricked into seeing a complete picture instead of lines. "Capturing light in a bottle" was how he thought of it— using electricity, not a machine with moving parts inside.

Philo's grin was wide. He told the idea to his father, who tried to understand but couldn't keep up with his son.

In the autumn Philo started high school, riding horseback four miles each way.

Mr. Tolman, the senior chemistry teacher, noticed that this freshman devoured books the way other students ate popcorn. He started tutoring Philo, coming in early and leaving late.

One day Mr. Tolman passed by a study hall and heard loud talking. Philo's latest hero was Albert Einstein, with his controversial new theory of relativity. Now Philo stood at the front of the room, enthusiastically explaining it to his classmates, step by step.

Usually Philo spoke little, with a halting voice. But when he could share his knowledge of science, he was a different boy.

Philo had been aching to discuss the idea he'd gotten in the potato field with someone who might understand. One day he finally told Mr. Tolman. All over the blackboard, he drew diagrams of his television.

His teacher was boggled. Philo ripped a page out of the notebook he always kept in his shirt pocket. He scribbled a diagram of an all-electric camera, the kind of converter he envisioned. An Image Dissector, he called it.

Mr. Tolman pointed out that it would take a lot of money to build such a thing. The only way he could think of helping was to encourage Philo to go on to college.

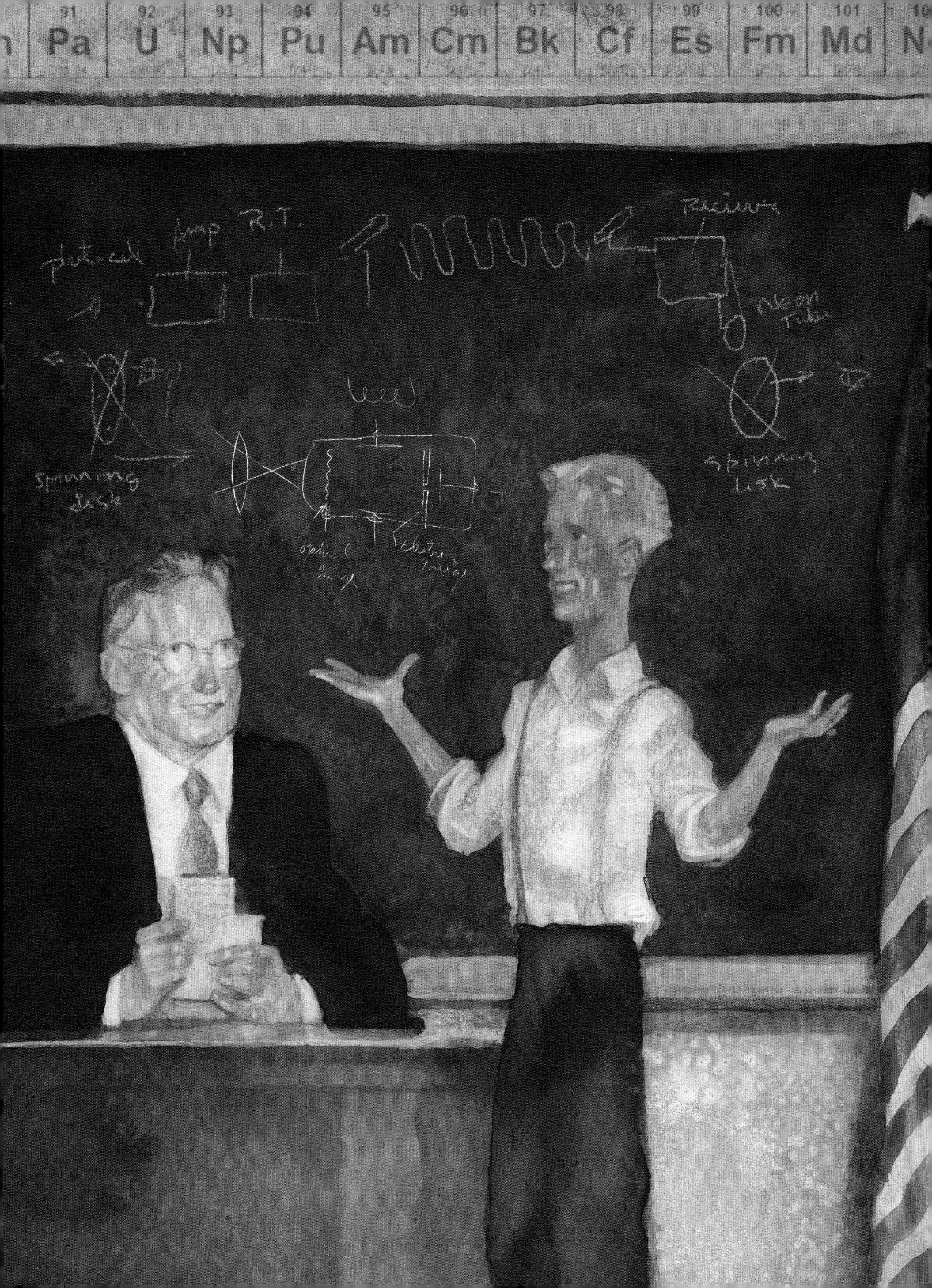

91 Pa
92 U
93 Np
94 Pu
95 Am
96 Cm
97 Bk
98 Cf
99 Es
100 Fm
101 Md
R.T.

But Philo was forced to quit college at eighteen, after his father died. By then the family had moved back to Utah, to the town of Provo, and Philo supported them by working at all sorts of jobs in nearby Salt Lake City.

His favorite one was repairing radios. Though commercial radio broadcasts had started four years earlier, Philo couldn't believe, in 1924, how many people still hadn't heard one. On weekends he organized "radio parties" so his friends could gather around one of the bulky wooden cabinets and listen to the new stations.

Pem Gardner, the girl next door, was interested in radio—and also in Philo.

Wasn't it funny, Philo remarked to Pem, how they liked to watch the radio even though there was nothing to see? Radio was such a fine way to bring folks together. And television, he sensed, would be even better.

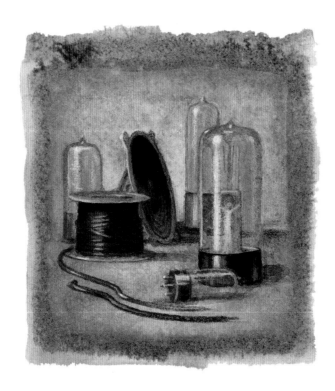

Thanks to his obsession with television, Philo had already lost one girlfriend, who called him too much of a dreamer. But Pem cheered him on. Now what he needed was money. He grew a mustache to look older, bought a new blue suit, and started to call himself Phil.

He met two California businessmen, and over dinner one night, he took them through a step-by-step explanation of his Image Dissector: a camera tube that would dissect an image into a stream of electrons, converting them into pulses of electrical current. A receiver would capture the current, then convert it back into points of light—the original image.

As he talked, he got more and more passionate. After scanning images line by line, just like rows in a potato field, this machine would beam them into homes. That was the best thing about television, he said—it would let families and whole communities share the same stories. By making people less ignorant of one another, he went on, it would teach and inspire. Maybe even lead to world peace.

The two businessmen exchanged looks, then agreed to put up $6,000 so Philo could build the first model. They gave him a year to make it work.

Philo hit upon a way to work twenty-four hours a day: he set himself problems to solve while sleeping.

He filed for several government patents that would protect his ideas for the next seventeen years. It was important to him to keep control, to get credit.

On their wedding night, he turned to Pem. "I have to tell you, there is another woman in my life—and her name is Television."

Pem helped out. Their first lab was their dining room table in Hollywood. Pem learned to use a precision welder to make tube elements— everything had to be built from scratch. When they needed a break, they went to one of the new talking movies.

Finally they got the lights, wires, and tubes to work in unison. But at the first demonstration, Philo forgot one item. He failed to take the power surge into account. The entire Image Dissector exploded. Pem, who took notes about everything, labeled this experiment "Bang! Pop! Sizzle!"

Still, Philo was able to find new investors, who gave him another year.

At his new lab in San Francisco, Philo met the deadline. In 1927, a small group of people watched as the first image in history flickered on a TV.

He said, "That's it, folks. We've done it—there you have electronic television."

That first image was not fancy. It was a straight line, blurry and bluish. Later he was able to show a dollar sign, and then the motion of cigarette smoke.

The first person to be televised was his true love, Pem, who didn't know she was on camera and had her eyes closed.

The following year, in front of a crowd of reporters, twenty-two-year-old Philo Farnsworth announced the invention of television.

That night he was behind the wheel of a borrowed car. He and Pem were heading home after catching a movie with another couple. They stopped to buy the *San Francisco Chronicle* from a newsboy. And there was a photo of Philo holding his invention. The article praised a "young genius" for creating a "revolutionary light machine."

Pem and his friends read it aloud, bouncing up and down, yelling. Philo was silent, but a big smile crossed his face.

He was a real inventor, like his heroes—someone who connected people, a shaper of the world to come. Thanks to him, the future would include **TV**.

AUTHOR'S NOTE

With his brainstorm in the potato field, Philo Farnsworth may have won the race to invent TV. But he lost the war over getting credit for it during his lifetime. Partly this was due to several strokes of bad luck, partly it was because he was more brilliant at inventing than at business. Mostly it was due to the Radio Corporation of America, the most powerful electronics company in the world in the 1930s. Farnsworth fought a heroic fight but never fully understood what he was up against. RCA was able to invest $50 million in the development of TV.

The company offered to pay Farnsworth for his idea, but surprisingly enough he refused—he wanted to keep control. With teams of lawyers, RCA started a patent war, stating that its employee Vladimir Zworykin had invented the all-electronic television system, that the idea of a teenage boy coming up with it was just silly. Then Justin Tolman, Philo's proud high school teacher, came forward with that old notebook drawing. In 1934 the U.S. Patent Office awarded priority of invention to Farnsworth.

RCA simply disregarded the ruling and debuted TV in 1939, at the World's Fair in New York City. RCA beamed its TV signal from atop the Empire State Building and broadcast speeches by President Franklin Roosevelt and Albert Einstein. Farnsworth was not mentioned. With a huge stomachache, he watched the demonstration on a television set in a department store window.

Two years later, when America entered World War II, commercial use of TV was banned, with all technology directed at defense. After the war ended in 1945, TV was slow to take off—there wasn't much to watch. Farnsworth's patents expired, and anyone was free to use his ideas. By 1949 one million sets had been sold, mostly by RCA. By 1955 an estimated half of the population of America simultaneously watched the grand opening of Disneyland on TV. Over the years, inventors continued to refine TV—for example, images today are digital, not made up of lines.

Farnsworth never stopped getting brainstorms, going on to receive 150 more patents. Trying to improve people's lives, he attacked problems on a global scale—he worked on controlling deadly viruses, safely disposing of waste, finding a source of cheap power.

Ill and bitter, he rarely watched TV and wouldn't let his sons watch. "Too many cowboy movies," he said. In 1969, with the televised landing of an American spacecraft on the moon, he and just about every American watched this historic event at the same time. Only then did he feel that TV was becoming the worthwhile machine he'd envisioned.

He died of pneumonia two years later, at age sixty-four, all but forgotten. His epitaph reads, "He loved his fellow man." Pem, who dedicated the rest of her life to making sure he got recognition, died in 2006 at age ninety-eight.

In recent years, several biographies and a Broadway play have finally helped establish Philo Farnsworth's rightful place in the history of American inventors.

SOURCES

(*especially for young readers)

BOOKS

*Calabro, Marian. *Zap! A Brief History of Television*. New York: Four Winds Press, 1992.

Farnsworth, Elma G. *Distant Vision: Romance and Discovery on an Invisible Frontier*. Salt Lake City: Pemberly Kent Publishers, 1990.

Godfrey, Donald G. *Philo T. Farnsworth: The Father of Television*. Salt Lake City: University of Utah Press, 2001.

*McCutcheon, Marc. *The Kid Who Named Pluto and the Stories of Other Extraordinary Young People in Science*. San Francisco: Chronicle Books, 2004.

*Roberts, Russell. *Philo T. Farnsworth: The Life of Television's Forgotten Inventor*. Hockessin, DE: Mitchell Lane Publishers, 2003.

Schatzkin, Paul. *The Boy Who Invented Television*. Burtonsville, MD: TeamCom Books, 2002.

Schwartz, Evan I. *The Last Lone Inventor: A Tale of Genius, Deceit, and the Birth of Television*. New York: HarperCollins Publishers, 2002.

Stashower, Daniel. *The Boy Genius and the Mogul: The Untold Story of Television*. New York: Broadway Books, 2002.

WEB SITES AND TELEVISION

Collins, Matthew, and Rocky Collins. "Big Dream, Small Screen," *American Experience* series. VHS. Boston: WGBH/PBS, 1997.

The Farnsworth Archives, www.philotfarnsworth.com.

"How Television Works," www.howstuffworks.com:80/tv.htm.

"How TV Works," The Institute of Electrical and Electronics Engineers Virtual Museum, www.ieee-virtual-museum.org/collection/tech.php?id=2345802&lid=1.

Television History: The First 75 Years, www.tvhistory.tv/Philo.htm.

PRIZE WINNING
RECIPES FROM THE
1981 NATIONAL
BEEF
COOK-OFF

AT SIOUX FALLS, SO. DAKOTA